FENG SHUI
for the New Millennium

A PRACTICAL GUIDE TO HARMONIOUS MODERN LIVING

Vincent Koh

⊥ ASIAPAC • SINGAPORE

Note to the reader
The author and publisher cannot accept responsibility for any outcome resulting from the unguided practice of any of the principles set out in this book.

Publisher
ASIAPAC BOOKS PTE LTD
996 Bendemeer Road #06-09
Singapore 339944
Tel: (65) 6392 8455
Fax: (65) 6392 6455
Email: asiapacbooks@pacific.net.sg

Come visit us at our Internet home page
www.asiapacbooks.com

First published October 2001
5th edition September 2007

© 2001 ASIAPAC BOOKS, SINGAPORE
ISBN 13   978-981-229-249-0
ISBN 10   981-229-249-7

Cover design by Illusion Creative Studio
Body text in 12pt Garamond
Printed in Singapore by Chung Printing Pte Ltd

Publisher's Note

Today, *Feng Shui* is getting increasingly popular and is rapidly gaining acceptance around the world. It is practised not just by older generations of Chinese, but also by the ultra-hip and highly-educated set. In fact, it is being faithfully practised even in the chic eateries, nightspots and boutiques of the West.

Feng Shui is not just another passing fad, to be discarded when interest has worn off. *Feng Shui* aficionados are signing up for courses to learn more about this esoteric art. However, one problem that has constantly plagued first-timers is the difficulty involved in putting principles into practice.

Asiapac Books is proud to present this little treasure trove of practical *Feng Shui* tips. Comprising snippets of *Feng Shui* ideas that can be easily implemented, this book will take its place among the essential literature of *Feng Shui*. We have no doubt veterans and novices alike will welcome this new work.

We would like to express our heartfelt thanks to Vincent Koh for generously sharing his treasury of *Feng Shui* tips with us, Lim Meng Hua for his witty illustrations, as well as the production team for their best efforts in putting this book together.

About the Author

Vincent Koh is a graduate in Marketing from the Chartered Institute of Marketing (UK). He is a successful businessman and has been in the building industry since 1967. In the course of business, he developed an interest in Feng Shui. His enthusiasm in Feng Shui has made him spend many years in pursuit of this art and he has conducted continuous research under the guidance of several experts in this field. He is also the founder of Singapore Feng Shui Centre and is currently the first to conduct certified Feng Shui courses in English at Singapore Polytechnic.

Today, he has become one of the most respected Feng Shui consultants providing clients with expert advice on Feng Shui layout design for their offices, shops, houses and apartments. The success of his clients speaks well of his expertise. To date, he has written four books — *Hsia Calendar, Feng Shui for the New Millennium, Unveil Your Destiny* and *Basic Science of Feng Shui* — published by Asiapac Books Pte Ltd. He frequently shares his knowledge through various media and also holds numerous talks and seminars on this subject.

The author can be contacted at:
Singapore Feng Shui Centre
Address:　10 Ubi Crescent #04-66 Ubi Techpark
　　　　　Singapore 408564
Tel:　　　(65) 6747 8226
Fax:　　　(65) 6747 8020
Email:　　singfc@fengshui.com.sg
Website:　www.fengshui.com.sg

Foreword

This book on practical *Feng Shui* tips came about by chance when I met up with Ms Lim Li Kok of Asiapac Books Pte Ltd. She gave me the inspiration to write this book for the new millennium.

After the successful launch of my first book *Hsia Calendar*, Li Kok suggested that I should continue to write and share what I know about *Feng Shui*. My knowledge and experience in applying the secrets of Chinese wisdom for health, wealth and harmony will enable readers to make optimum use of this ancient art in their home or workplace.

The primary objective of writing *Feng Shui for the New Millennium* is to arouse readers' interest in *Feng Shui* so that they can appreciate and further explore this mystical science.

I realise that writing in depth on this subject can get very technical. This is especially so when it involves difficult and complex formulae which readers may find rather complicated and hard to digest. As such, I have presented my knowledge in point form and spiced them up with many witty illustrations.

Feng Shui is a study which reveals the essence of Chinese cosmology and metaphysics. Uncertainties and risks abound in daily life. This book will help readers to comprehend the practical aspects of *Feng Shui*, so that they too can apply these methods to meet their own needs.

My vision is to guide readers into the world of *Feng Shui*. This book is not about superstition. Rather, it focuses on the underlying principles and philosophy behind *Feng Shui*, so that we can be aware of the invisible energies that exist in the environment.

This illustrated guidebook is meant to be a user-friendly supplement to all the formulae and techniques used in *Feng Shui* practice. Contained in this simple yet comprehensive handbook are write-ups and illustrations on the practical aspects of *Feng Shui*, as well as an overview of the benefits brought about by it, including good health, prosperity and harmony.

I hope all my students and readers will find these *Feng Shui* tips useful and invaluable. Who knows, it may pinpoint the problems currently troubling you. Put the art of *Feng Shui* to the test by incorporating it into your daily life today.

Vincent Koh

Contents

PART I:
INTRODUCTION

The Art of Living

✔ According to traditional Chinese thought, our life is influenced by many factors. Listed below are five of them.

Destiny

✔ Destiny is the inheritance of, and influence by, conditions already determined at our birth.

✔ Though we cannot change our destiny, we can predict the timing of events and adapt to circumstances accordingly. If the weather report forecasts rain, we can bring an umbrella. If it is windy, we can put on a windbreaker. Likewise, if our destiny does not seem rosy, we can look to geomancy for help.

✔ Compiled by the Chinese thousands of years ago, the *Hsia Calendar* enables us to erect a person's Four Pillars of Destiny with information like the year, month, day and hour of his birth.

✔ The Four Pillars of Destiny is a scientific tool used by the Chinese since ancient times to reveal the cosmic components of each person. In this method, our birth data is expressed as a composition of the Five Elements — Metal, Water, Wood, Fire and Earth.

✔ Our Four Pillars of Destiny consists of two elements each, therefore making a total of eight elements, or what we call the Eight Characters. From these eight elements, we can determine whether our Self Element is Metal, Water, Wood, Fire or Earth.

✔ Our destiny can be revealed by assessing the strength and weakness of these elements and how they interact with one another. Knowing the strength and weakness of our Self Element, we can use favourable colour schemes and directions to enhance our destiny.

Luck

✔ Our destiny and luck cycle can be revealed by analysing the interactions amongst the components of our birth data.

✔ Luck refers to variations in our fortune — the ups and downs in our life. If we address the factors that control our luck, we can moderate the downs and maximise the ups and even transform a poor fate into a successful one.

Feng Shui

✔ *Feng Shui* is the art of living in harmony with the environment. It is also about how the environment conditions us and how we, in turn, influence our environment.

✔ Knowing the factors that control our luck, we can enhance them with *Feng Shui*. But if our luck is down, *Feng Shui* can buffer the hard knocks and rude shocks that come our way.

Philanthropy

✔ There is a cause and effect for our every action. If we create more good causes, we can change our *karma* and thereby improve our destiny.

Education

✔ Education opens the door to opportunities for a better life. It teaches us to acquire knowledge, a commodity of utmost importance in this information age. Learning is a lifelong process, and helps us become a better person.

Feng Shui

✔ There are various definition of *Feng Shui*. Literally *"Feng"* means wind and *"Shui"* refers to water. These are the two most significant features in Chinese geomancy.

✔ *Feng* does not merely refer to wind and air, but also to an abstract and intangible energy. Wind travels along the contour of the landscape and dissipates in water. If this energy is positive, it will interact with water to give *Sheng Qi*, or benign energy. *Sha Qi*, or "killing" energy, travels in straight lines and is detrimental because it "kills" your luck.

✔ Wind carries energy into our house through doors, windows, chimneys and air vents.

✔ In the modern world, *Shui* includes water not just in rivers and seas, but also in man-made reservoirs, pipes and drains.

✔ In modern cities, *Shui* also refers to roads, streets, highways and railway lines. Thus, it encompasses the tangible, physical aspect of our environment.

✔ The Chinese had discovered that wind and water carry the invisible life energy *Qi*. These natural forces exist in our surroundings and have a significant impact on our habitat.

✔ These abstract forces move dynamically to a predictable pattern. They can influence us in positive and negative ways.

✔ For example, if our door directly faces a straight road or a narrow corridor, it will be exposed to *Sha Qi*. Knowing *Feng Shui* principles will enable us to overcome the *Sha Qi*.

✔ The study of *Feng Shui* aims to find ways to make use of good influences and avoid the bad ones in our environment. Putting *Feng Shui* to good use in our residence or workplace will help to create a harmonious, healthy and prosperous environment.

Feng Shui Analysis for Our Home

Purpose of a Feng Shui Analysis

✔ To select a prosperous site for building a house.

✔ To select the best orientation for a house.

✔ To select the best unit within an apartment block.

✔ To discover the energy relating to the specific birth data and elements of each occupant, and select appropriate rooms for everyone.

✔ To discover the movement of energies through our house.

✔ To make the best decisions in interior design.

✔ To maintain long-term prosperity through regular checks.

✔ To forecast any cyclical changes in the environment.

Signs that a Feng Shui Analysis is Needed

✔ Family members encounter unexpected events like accidents.

✔ Quarrels erupt frequently among family members.

✔ Your steady job is suddenly threatened, or business slows down and sales drop.

✔ Health and sleep problems besiege family members.

✔ Children's studies deteriorate.

Feng Shui and You

✔ *Feng Shui* links up, and interacts with, the following:
  • The movement of *Qi*
  • The characteristics of *Yin* and *Yang*
  • The Five Elements — Metal, Wood, Water, Fire and Earth
  • Chinese astrology

✔ It enables you to organise your home to facilitate energy movement and avoid energy clustering or energy acceleration within the house.

✔ You can tap *Sheng Qi* and disperse, disrupt or remove *Sha Qi*.

✔ Good *Feng Shui* can bring good health, harmonious relations and prosperity to the occupants of the home. It also harnesses and enhances environmental *Qi* to improve the flow of *Qi* within our bodies, thus improving our life.

✔ This concept holds true in factories and offices too.

✔ In business premises, good *Feng Shui* creates opportunities for business growth and profit-making.

✔ On the contrary, bad *Feng Shui* features create disharmony and loss of opportunities.

✔ Bad *Feng Shui* can even lead to tragic consequences.

Hsia Calendar

✔ The *Hsia Calendar* runs parallel to the Lunar and Solar Calendars.

Excerpt from *Hsia Calendar* by Vincent Koh

✔ In the Solar Calendar, a new year commences on 1st January and ends on 31st December.

✔ Though the Lunar Calendar also has 12 months, the first day of the year commences on the first day of the Chinese Lunar New Year. This day varies from year to year but generally occurs in late January or early February.

✔ The *Hsia Calendar* commences on the first day of Spring, usually around 4th or 5th February.

✔ The *Hsia Calendar* is no ordinary calendar. With it, we can express a person's birth data in the form of Four Pillars, each representing the year, month, day and hour. Each pillar is represented by a pair of elements called Heavenly Stem and Earthly Branch.

✔ These Four Pillars of Destiny are also known as Eight Characters (八字). Based on these Eight Characters, an expert in destiny analysis will be able to analyse a person's character, luck cycle and family relationships. The *Hsia Calendar* is thus an essential tool in destiny analysis.

✔ It can also be used for selecting an auspicious date and time for a wedding ceremony, the grand opening of a new store or moving into a new home.

✔ Today, the West has already started to take an interest in this classic, developed over 4,000 years ago by the Chinese.

PART II:
PRACTICAL FENG SHUI IDEAS

Chapter 1

Landscape —
Basic Feng Shui Concepts

Qi

✔ *Qi* is the breath essential to maintaining environmental, physical and emotional balance.

✔ Each of us possesses *Qi*. Its characteristics and the way in which it moves differ from person to person.

✔ There are three different kinds of *Qi*.
  - One that circulates in the atmosphere, as when a pathway meanders through a garden.

  - One that circulates in the ground, as when a river winds gently across a landscape.

  - One that circulates within our body, as when a *Tai Ji* master executes his move in an unhurried manner.

✔ Wind currents carry energy into the house. This energy will be auspicious if the flow is slow and meandering.

✔ A straight and rapid flow of *Qi* carries *Sha Qi,* that is, poison arrows.

Sheng Qi

Sha Qi

✔ Avoid having too many sharp corners as they will act as obstacles to this flow of energy and prevent you from attaining your goals in life.

Celestial Creatures

✔ Dragons, tigers and other celestial creatures featured in the language of *Feng Shui* are to be construed in a symbolic sense.

✔ The four Celestial Creatures — Green Dragon, White Tiger, Red Phoenix and Black Tortoise — refer to the landscape surrounding our house.

The Ideal Landscape

✔ The Green Dragon hills to the East represent the central requirement of good landscape.

✔ The White Tiger hills to the West should merge with the Green Dragon hills to create auspicious *Qi*.

✔ The Red Phoenix landscape to the South should be an open space that is low-lying and flat, signifying a life of ease and luxury.

✔ The Black Tortoise range of hills to the North gives support and protection.

Locating the Celestial Creatures

✔ Look out from your main door. On your left is the Green Dragon and on the right is your White Tiger. The front of your house is called the Red Phoenix and the back of your house is referred to as the Black Tortoise.

Green Dragon and White Tiger

✔ The Dragon symbolises *Yang* and represents power.

✔ The Tiger symbolises *Yin* and represents negative qualities.

✔ Look out of your main door. If the house on your left is higher than the house on your right, it means the Dragon is controlling the Tiger. This is auspicious.

✔ On the other hand, if the house on your right is higher than the house on your left, it is regarded as inauspicious, for the Dragon is suppressed by the Tiger.

Red Phoenix and Black Tortoise
✔ The Red Phoenix refers to the front of the house, which should be an open space to symbolise wealth.

✔ The Black Tortoise refers to the back of the house. It should have a strong support to symbolise stability and strength.

✔ The main door should not be blocked, and should preferably face an open ground. It is good if the front of the house faces a pool of water, a gentle slope or a playground.

✔ This open ground, representing water, should be lower than the house.

✔ The back of the house, symbolising support, should be higher than the house.

✔ Tall buildings can substitute for mountains and can give good support to the house.

✔ A solid rear boundary wall is also acceptable as support.

✔ Hedges and trees behind the house can act as support if the branches are not overgrown.

Water Dragon

✔ *Feng Shui* suggests that a house should be backed by a mountain, with the front facing a pond, stream or river.

✔ This body of water in front of your house is referred to as a Water Dragon.

✔ The water is responsible for attracting and accumulating quality *Qi*.

✔ An artificial waterway or drain can be utilised as a Water Dragon in place of a pond, stream or river.

Chapter 2

Site — Your Surroundings

Orientation

✔ House orientation is an important consideration. A house that has its back to a mountain and looks down a gentle slope, pond or playground is desirable.

✔ For high-rise apartment, the entrance to the lobby is the facing of the building and the door into your flat is the facing of your home. Both doors have different *Feng Shui* implications. See page 97 for further elaboration.

Water

✔ It is usually auspicious to have water at the front of the house as it can bring more opportunities into your life. In land-scarce regions, an open courtyard or garden can substitute for water.

✔ The quality of water is important. It should be alive, clean and active. Stagnant and murky water indicates tainted *Qi* and is inauspicious.

River

✔ Roads and rivers are pathways of energy and can conduct, gather and disperse energy according to their flow pattern.

✔ If a house faces a river, this is good as the family will enjoy wealth. A house facing away from a river is less fortunate. Residents will see opportunities but will not be able to grasp them.

✔ A river flowing towards the front door of the house is good. However, if it flows away, the residents will suffer financial losses.

Road

✔ In *Feng Shui*, roads are evaluated in the same way as rivers.

✔ The flow of a road is equivalent to the flow of water in a river.

✔ A road that encircles a house like a noose is harmful to the occupants.

✔ A house situated between two parallel roads should be avoided. It is as if the roads are "squeezing" the house.

✔ If a road running in front of the house is higher than the floor level, problems will befall the residents.

✔ Gently curved roads and paths that follow natural contours are best suited for carrying smooth *Qi* flow.

✔ However, roads that curve towards a house are destructive as the flow of *Qi* along the road will cut through the house like a knife.

✔ Likewise, straight roads or paths pointing directly at your entrance are potentially dangerous.

✔ Straight roads that lead traffic rushing towards your house creates physical *Sha Qi*. The intensity of the *Sha Qi* increases if the road slopes down to your house.

✔ If the main door cannot be relocated, place a screen outside the door to ward off *Sha Qi*.

✔ Houses near bridges, elevated highways and bus interchanges are buffeted by destructive energy.

T-junction Road
✔ Danger can befall a house facing a T-junction if the road facing the house is too steep.

✔ The headlights of on-coming vehicles can disturb occupants at night, causing restlessness.

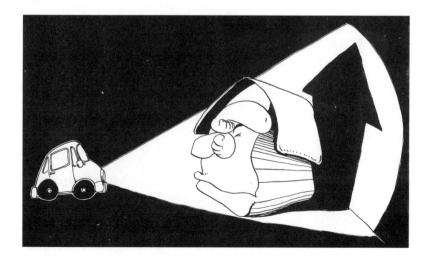

✔ It is difficult for *Sheng Qi* to reach the house furthest from the main road.

✔ Position your main gate and main door away from the main junction.

✔ Grow thick hedges to absorb the impact of *Sha Qi* coming from the T-junction.

✔ A tree planted outside your house can also absorb the impact of *Sha Qi* coming from the T-junction.

Playground
✔ A house facing a playground is better than one facing a tall building. However, a playground should be slightly lower than the ground level of the house.

✔ Alternatively, choose a house that faces an open ground or a swimming pool.

Bus-stop

✔ Avoid buying a house with a bus-stop just outside its main door.

✔ A bus-stop outside a commercial building is good though.

Place of Worship

✔ Avoid residing directly opposite a temple, church or mosque as such places exert a unique spiritual influence and is usually associated with *Yin* energy.

✔ The *Qi* emitted from such places where people seek help for their many problems is often strong and unpredictable. It is best to avoid them except for commercial purposes.

Cemetery

✔ Graveyards, funeral parlours and hospitals are regarded as having a high concentration of *Yin* energies associated with sickness and death. It is not ideal to live near these places. The living and the dead should not reside together.

House on a Cliff

✔ An isolated house atop a hill or cliff is vulnerable to various intangible forces, causing beneficial *Qi* to disperse quickly. In fact, a lonely house on a cliff will produce a widow.

✔ Houses built on a cliff give a sense of isolation and require the support of buildings, fences or trees to provide protection from adverse weather.

✔ Avoid constructing a house at the edge of a cliff, or your wealth will dwindle.

✔ Ideally, houses located on a cliff should have proper support behind them. A high range of hills behind is preferred.

✔ If the wind is harsh and ferocious, use partitions, screens or dividers to avoid being the target of destructive energies.

✔ Avoid a house near a road that has been cut into a hillside.

House by the Sea

✔ Houses that nestle against a hill, with a distant view of the sea, have a good *Feng Shui* configuration as compared to houses too close to the sea. The same reasoning applies to houses near lakes or rivers.

✔ Houses with the back facing the sea will bring family disharmony.

✔ Houses with a scenic view of calm water in front and a range of hills behind have a good *Feng Shui* composition.

✔ If the sea, river or lake contains foul-smelling, decaying materials, and is muddy or polluted, it will give off poisonous *Qi* which causes ill health.

Inauspicious Structure

✔ If your main door is facing a main road, your house will be noisy and polluted, especially if the traffic is heavy.

✔ A main door that is hit by the lethal energy of secret poison arrows cannot enjoy good *Feng Shui*.

✔ Make sure your front door is not blocked. Remove any obstructions near the door.

✔ Sharp objects that point at a house are harmful because they emit destructive energy.

✔ Look out for large tree branches pointing at your house, as well as the TV antenna on your neighbour's roof that directly faces your main door or bedroom windows. These will shoot poison arrows into your house.

✔ Structures that have a knife-like edge pointing at your house bring disaster. Avoid facing the sharp edges of houses opposite yours. Sharp edges cut off the *Sheng Qi* coming from that direction.

✔ To defend against your neighbour's sharp edges, place a plant in a strategic position to ward off the arrows charging at your door.

✔ Pitched roofs slope down for the purpose of easy drainage. Unfortunately, they resemble arrows. Avoid facing such pointed roofs as they will bring bad luck to you.

✔ Shiny objects directed at a house are also harmful. These include reflection of light from glass panels.

Pole

✔ If the front entrance of your house directly faces a pole, even if it faces a good direction, it is an unlucky house as your luck is blocked.

✔ A pole directly outside your house is more lethal than one across the road.

✔ It is also inauspicious to have a pole facing your window.

✔ A lamp post outside a house could distract the occupants inside, particularly if the light shines into the bedroom.

✔ Power lines can also be potent if they point directly at your front door or bedroom windows.

✔ If lamp posts, telegraphic poles, flag poles and bus-stops cannot be avoided, they should be shielded from your doors and windows.

Heavy Object

✔ Heavy objects like stones or statues, properly placed outside the main door, can help to stabilise an unsettling situation like disputes and scandals.

✔ Beware of sculptures that have irregular shapes and sharp features though.

No-entry sign

✔ A no-entry sign that directly faces your main door is a stumbling block to your progress.

Rubbish Compound

✔ A rubbish compound in front of the house will generate bad *Qi* flow. Even a good facing will be undermined by the foul air.

Drain

✔ Drains are related to your finances and your intestines, so make sure they are not blocked.

✔ Water from drains should not flow out near the main entrance.

✔ Drain water should flow out from the back of your house.

✔ If you have an open drain that flows out near your main entrance, cover it with drain gratings.

Sewer Manhole

✔ If you have a sewer manhole in your compound, place a potted plant over it or grow some small plants around it.

Step

✔ There should always be a step leading up to your house. Roads are regarded as rivers and if your house is below the level of the road, you are inviting danger.

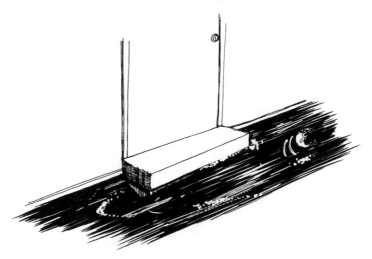

Wall

✔ A man-made wall running parallel to the main entrance of your house will create an obstacle and cause an imbalance of *Qi*. Your progress will be blocked.

✔ The perimeter walls should not be taller than your main door.

✔ The front wall should not be higher than the rear wall.

✔ Boundary walls should not be decorated with sharp spikes.

Pillar

✔ It is considered bad *Feng Shui* to have structural pillars blocking the way to the main door of a house. Place a screen between the pillars and the main door to prevent inauspicious *Qi* from penetrating the house.

✔ A house supported by pillars — for example, one with a ground-level garage below it — is considered unlucky because it does not rest on solid ground.

✔ You may build a wall from the ground to the soffit of the floor level for stability.

Back of a House

✔ If two houses have their backs too close to each other, the flow of *Qi* will be blocked.

✔ Avoid building the back wall too high, otherwise *Qi* cannot flow smoothly into the house.

✔ A house without a back door or window obstructs *Qi* from flowing smoothly into the house.

✔ The back door should not directly face the main door or *Qi* will leave the house swiftly.

✔ The back door should not be larger than the main door.

Garage

✔ The location of the garage is another aspect that should be considered carefully.

✔ Do not construct the master bedroom on top of the garage.

✔ It should not be located on the Tiger side of the house.

✔ Do not park your car right up by the front door. We think of cars as tigers. When you start the engine, it is like pumping pressure at the house.

✔ Avoid parking your car facing the main door.

Driveway

✔ A driveway leading from the main road to the house should be smooth, meandering and relatively level on approach.

✔ A driveway that narrows at the foot (near the gate) signifies dwindling career and financial opportunities. The worst of all situations is if it also slopes down.

Shape of Land

✔ A rectangular or square piece of land is best.

✔ L-shaped or U-shaped arrangements are not favourable.

✔ Irregular shapes can bring trouble, and attention is needed.

✔ If the plot is large, the backyard can be slightly higher than the front.

✔ If the garden is small, it is best to have it level rather than sloping.

Shape of Building
✔ Rectangular and square shapes are best.

✔ Do not design a building with a missing corner. Alternatively, extend the depth of the missing corner with mirrors.

✔ When considering an irregular shape or a stylish design, make sure the flow of *Qi* entering the building is not affected.

✔ The shape and design of a building should blend in with the surrounding buildings. It should neither be too tall nor too low.

Chapter 3

In the Home

Front Door

✔ The front door should be the same size as or slightly larger than all others. It should open inwardly so that *Qi* gets channelled into the house rather than out of it.

✔ Your front door should open into the main part of the room, not into a wall. Opening a door into a wall will stop the *Qi* from entering the house.

✔ The front door should be slightly higher than the patio outside.

✔ It is inauspicious if the foyer level is higher than the front door level.

✔ A single-panelled door is better than a double-panelled one.

✔ A double-panelled door should have panels of equal size.

✔ Door should be solid, so louvre doors are not recommended.

Door Bell

✔ Mechanical bells vibrate in such a way that they cleanse the atmosphere when they chime. Make sure you like the sound.

Security Alarm

✔ A security alarm is installed to keep away unwelcomed intruders.

✔ A faulty alarm causes noise disturbance to the surrounding energies and is considered inauspicious.

✔ Make sure your alarm is checked and serviced regularly by a professional.

Hallway

✔ You should have bright lights in the hallway. It should be uncluttered with enough space to move freely from one room to another.

✔ A dark and cluttered hallway accumulates stagnant and negative energy.

✔ A hallway should not be long and narrow, as it will "squeeze" *Qi* and can turn it from a beneficial energy to an unstable one.

✔ A long hallway should have windows on at least one side for *Qi* to circulate.

Staircase

✔ If a staircase leads straight down to the front door, *Qi* will be drawn out the door without circulating through the house.

✔ A spiral staircase can damage your health, especially if it is in the middle of the house.

✔ It is better for an apartment's main door to face a staircase leading to an upper floor than to face a staircase that leads down. A staircase that leads down symbolises a drop in status.

Window

✔ Windows are related to your eyes. Keep them sparkling clean and replace any cracked glass immediately. Cracked glass is a bad omen in *Feng Shui*.

✔ Beware of any sharp, pointed objects facing the window. Sharp edges give off negative energies and should be avoided.

✔ If a window opens out to a view with *Sha Qi*, keep the window closed or hang a curtain as a shield.

Column

✔ Interior columns play an important role in the *Feng Shui* of a house.

✔ Round columns are better than square ones.

✔ Square columns have sharp angles that point in a threatening manner at the residents.

✔ A good way to neutralise the sharp edges of a column is to install mirrors on all sides of the column, camouflaging the column effectively.

Ceiling

✔ Ceilings should be high and well-lit.

✔ Low ceilings in a confined space will cause depression and headaches.

✔ Uneven and low ceilings should be avoided.

✔ Exposed beams can be concealed with a suspended ceiling.

Number

✔ House number should be hung above eye level and in line if there are two or more numbers.

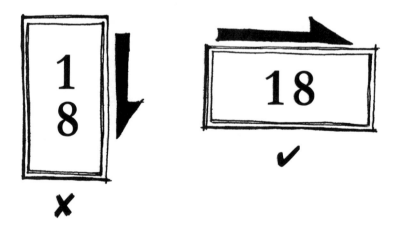

✔ The Chinese are sometimes prepared to pay a high price bidding for auspicious numbers. To them, 9 is a lucky number that symbolises the fullness of Heaven and Earth. The number 8 is considered extremely auspicious because it sounds like the Cantonese word for prosperity.

✔ In *Feng Shui* analysis, the number 7 is the current ruling number from Year 1984 to Year 2003. Thus, it is considered the most auspicious number during this era.

✔ The numbers 5 and 2 are regarded as sickness and misfortune in Flying Star Feng Shui and should be avoided.

Colour

✔ Colour is associated with the Five Elements. To create harmony in your home, it is important to know the interactions of the Five Elements. You can then choose your most favourable colour scheme that corresponds to the element which is most auspicious for you. See page 91 for further elaboration on the Five Elements.

✔ Colours are related to the Five Elements and their properties in different ways.

- Red, Purple - Fire
- Blue, Black - Water
- White, Gold - Metal
- Green - Wood
- Brown - Earth

✔ Colour schemes can enhance our home when correctly applied to interior decoration or the selection of paintings, wallpapers, curtains, carpets and bed sheets.

✔ Selection of colours should complement the birth data of each family member. For example, use blue to enhance the Water Element of your home and counteract the strong Metal Element.

Painting
✔ Decorative paintings can enhance the *Feng Shui* of your house.

✔ Paintings of mountainous landscape symbolise Black Tortoise support.

✔ Scenic paintings of rivers, fountains and waterfalls are suitable for enhancing the wealth and prosperity corner.

✔ Paintings of flowers like peonies and roses in the romance sector activates passion and romance.

Wind Chime

✔ A wind chime slows down energy by creating a little obstacle to it.

✔ Hang it high up to slow down the flow of energy and prevent unexpected events beyond your control from happening.

✔ A wind chime is commonly used to dissolve the *Sha Qi* of Five Yellow, an inauspicious star which causes disharmony and misfortunes. In the year 2000, Five Yellow is in the North.

✔ Careful placement of the wind chime is necessary. Hanging it in the wrong location may attract ghosts or spirits.

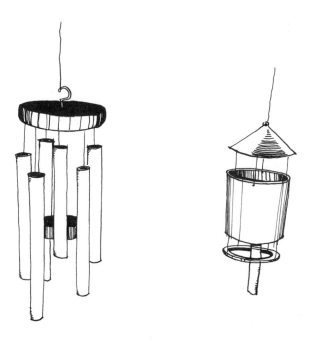

Curtain

✔ Hang curtains at your windows rather than blinds as they are softer.

✔ Curtains can act as a shield to deflect external *Sha Qi*.

✔ Light-coloured curtains are better as they allow some daylight to penetrate into the house.

Screen and Divider

✔ Screens or dividers are excellent for creating regular-shaped sections in your house.

✔ Choose screens that are decorated with auspicious objects, but avoid screens that are decorated with angular designs.

✔ Do not display your screen in a zig-zag fashion. They create too many sharp edges that emit *Sha Qi*.

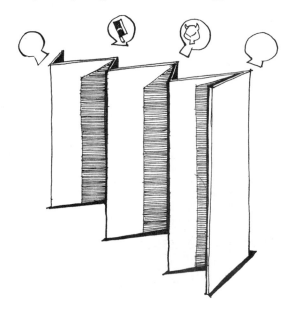

✔ Screens or dividers should be firmly anchored to the floor or suspended from the ceiling.

Shelving
✔ Shelving with straight, sharp edges and pointed corners produce harmful *Qi*.

✔ Position all shelving as low as possible to prevent the feeling of knife blades stabbing you.

✔ Sitting with your back against a sharp-edged shelf is best avoided.

✔ Alternatively, cover it with a cloth or curtain to ward off the threatening *Qi*.

Dining Table
✔ Square or rectangular dining tables have sharp corners. Do not sit at the corner edge of a square or rectangular table. It creates the effect of arrows pointing towards you. Round or oval tables are preferred.

Mirror

✔ Use mirrors that have a good reflective surface. Tarnished mirrors cannot deflect *Sha Qi* effectively.

✔ A small, round and convex mirror has the effect of reflecting and spreading *Qi*. Other objects with a reflective surface will create a similar effect.

✔ The careful orientation of mirrors can make a room appear more spacious, especially if you can reflect the garden or water into the house.

✔ Large mirrors can be used to give the impression that a room extends into a missing corner.

✔ If several mirrors are joined together, the reflection will seem disjointed.

✔ Mirrors need to be large enough and positioned such that they reflect the occupants' heads in full.

✔ If you have mirrors in your bedroom, position them such that they do not face your bed.

✔ While we sleep, our bodies emit *Qi*. This is part of a cleansing process. A mirror facing the bed may reflect this *Qi* back to you.

✔ If you already have a mirror facing the bed, cover the mirror with a cloth or shift the bed so that it will not face the mirror.

✔ Having a mirror in the dining area is excellent, because it is believed that the doubling of food at the dining table is auspicious.

✔ Remember that cracked mirrors need to be replaced immediately.

Prayer Altar

✔ The altar is respected as the most sacred object in the house, and it should be located in the sector most favourable to the owner.

✔ Avoid placing a prayer altar in the bedroom.

✔ The altar should be kept neat and tidy at all times.

✔ Place the altar in a bright corner facing the main door or balcony.

Flower

✔ Dried flowers are dead flowers. They emit too much *Yin* energy and does not contribute to good *Feng Shui*. Artificial flowers are better than dried flowers.

✔ Artificial silk flowers may be used as substitutes for fresh flowers. Since artificial flowers do not turn brown or shed their petals, you will not be confronted by symbols of aging and death. However, they are not as effective as real ones.

✔ Placement of artificial flowers in the romance sector can also help to enhance your romance star.

Plant

✔ What we smell upon entering a house can affect how we perceive it. The pleasant fragrance given off by plants in the home is desirable. Incense is also a good source of fragrance.

✔ Plants are a wonderful producer of healthy *Qi* in the house. However, withered and dying plants produce negative energy and should be replaced immediately.

Fish

✔ Fish may be used to enhance and stimulate good energy. Ideally, goldfish are recommended for the home.

✔ A fish tank with six goldfish is ideal. It represents the Metal Element, which gives birth to Water, a symbol of wealth.

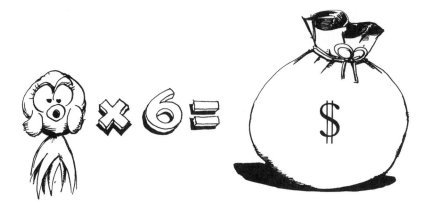

✔ Dead fish emit negative energy and should be replaced immediately.

Aquarium
✔ There are several techniques of activating the wealth location of a house. Keeping a tank of fish is one of the popular ways of enhancing the prosperity corners of a house.

✔ When a house does not enjoy a view of water, aquariums are installed to nourish a house with *Qi*.

✔ It is advisable to place the fish tank in the wealth and prosperity corner of the house.

Light
✔ Light is often employed by *Feng Shui* masters to improve luck.

✔ If you install lights to pillars on either side of the main gate to your driveway, it will bring more energy into your house.

✔ It is advisable not to install ceiling lamps with five bulbs. In *Feng Shui* theories, a five-bulb lamp represents *Sha Qi*.

✔ Activities carried out below lamps may cause unwarranted disturbances in the atmosphere and result in misfortunes.

Air-conditioner

✔ Avoid having an air-con fan coil over your head. It tends to stir *Qi* around your head. The condensation from the cold air is not good for you.

Fan

✔ Electric fans stimulate *Qi* circulation and deflect the overbearing force coming from long corridors.

Electrical Power Point

✔ The electrical system relates to your nervous system. Having too many overloaded plugs and exposed wires around your home can stress out your nervous system.

Temperature

✔ The temperature of your house should be more or less consistent throughout or it can create arguments and health problems.

Sitting Room

✔ If your sitting room is large enough, divide it into two areas — one for watching television and the other for chatting.

✔ Modern electrical appliances like televisions, rotating fans, hi-fi equipment and clocks can be placed in the wealth corner to stimulate money-generating *Qi*.

✔ Placing electrical appliances in the wrong location may cause problems to the residents.

✔ The ringing tone of a telephone can also be used as a *Feng Shui* tool to activate the wealth corner.

✔ A clock that chimes is also a good *Feng Shui* tool in the house.

✔ Consult a *Feng Shui* practitioner if you are not sure where the wealth corner of your sitting room is.

✔ Position your sofas such that they face the door rather than have their backs to it, so as to avoid the feeling of vulnerability.

✔ If your house is left empty most of the time, turn on the radio. This is one of the most efficient method of activating *Yang* energy in the house.

Master Bedroom
1. *Bed*
✔ You have to consider which room to use as your master bedroom, the direction that the bedroom door should face, and the direction that the bed should face.

✔ A bed needs a solid wall to give it good support. Placing the bed in the middle of the room is like floating in the air without firm support.

✔ Also, overcrowding of furniture in the bedroom deters *Qi* circulation and is undesirable.

2. *Lighting*
✔ Lights should not be hung directly over your head.

✔ Reading lights should be placed on either side of the bed, preferably with a dimmer control.

3. *Electrical Equipment*
✔ Do not place the television directly opposite the bed.

✔ Before you go to bed, remember to switch off the television, radio and computer.

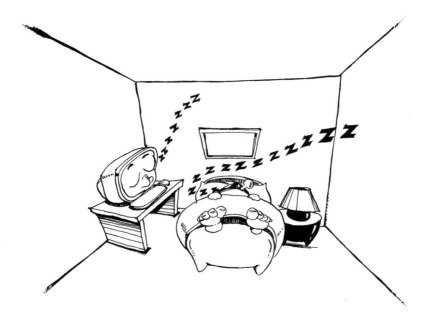

✔ The television set in the bedroom should be covered up, or else the magnetic field will charge at you when your body is at rest.

✔ As with all electrical appliances, a personal computer in the bedroom will give you an electrical charge while you are sleeping. Place a cover over it when not in use.

4. *Telephone*
✔ The ringing tone of your telephone should be low and mild.

✔ If you do not want to be rudely awakened by a call in the middle of your sleep, remember to switch off the phone before you go to bed.

5. ***Curtain***
    ✔ Curtains can act as a screen to fend off external *Sha Qi*.

    ✔ Draw the curtain if you want privacy.

    ✔ The colour of curtains should harmonise with your personal elements.

    ✔ Blinds and screens can also substitute for curtains.

6. ***Ventilation***
    ✔ In air-conditioned rooms, windows should be opened at least every other day to replace stale air with fresh air.

7. ***Attached Bathroom***
    ✔ Keep the door closed when not occupied.

    ✔ Do not place your bed directly opposite the toilet door.

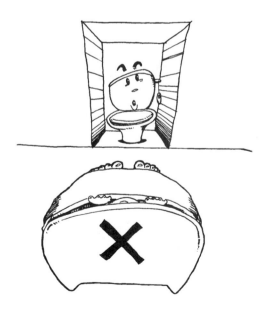

✔ The bathroom door should not directly face the bedroom door.

✔ Do not place a toilet bowl facing the toilet door.

✔ Remember to flush the toilet bowl before and after use.

✔ Keep the toilet bowl cover down after using.

8. **Window**

✔ Look out for unfavourable objects pointing directly into the room.

✔ Draw the curtain to avoid invasion of privacy.

✔ Avoid sleeping with your head facing the window.

9. **Beam**

✔ We need to pay attention to the positioning of exposed beams above us as they are the major cause of illness.

✔ Exposed and overhanging beams are oppressive structures that harm *Qi* flow.

✔ Do not sleep with a beam over your head. You will have to bear with the pressure exerted on you in your sleep.

✔ Moreover, sleeping with a beam over your head can be a source of headaches and migraines.

✔ Sleeping with a beam protruding over your stomach area can cause ulcers and intestinal problems.

✔ Sleeping with a beam over the foot of your bed may impair your mobility later on in life.

Children's Bedroom

✔ Place the bed in the most favourable corner.

✔ If a child does not excel in his studies, place a study table in his academic sector.

✔ You can also paint a favourable colour to enhance his element.

✔ Use white or bright, solid colours for the walls.

✔ Let the room be well-lit with no dark corners.

✔ The presence of books in the bedroom symbolises the acquisition of knowledge.

✔ Ensure rooms are clean and tidy everyday.

✔ Keep toys away in the cupboard and remove them when not in play anymore.

✔ Carry out spring cleaning at least twice a year.

Kitchen

✔ The kitchen should have an energy that is clean, fresh and bright.

✔ The stove should not be erected next to the wash basin as this will cause a "water and fire conflict".

✔ Knives send out cutting *Qi* and create arguments. Always keep them out of sight when not in use.

✔ The cooker is best situated in the East, South-East or South-

West sectors. The least auspicious is the North as it can lead to conflict, or the South as it can create intense Fire energy in the house.

✔ The stove should not face the main door as it will absorb the incoming *Qi*.

✔ The stove should not face the toilet door. If it is already there, keep the toilet door closed when not in use.

✔ A refrigerator is related to the Water Element and the stove is regarded as a Fire Element. If you place your refrigerator next to the stove, it is like dropping an ice-cube into a cup of hot coffee.

✔ Beams over the stove will cause financial losses.

✔ The kitchen should not be located in the middle of the house. The effect is like burning the heart of the house.

Chapter 4

The Garden

Tree

✔ Trees can be both good and bad in city *Feng Shui*.

✔ A tree outside your house can act as a shield to ward off negative *Qi* heading for your house, like traffic noise and air pollution.

✔ However, if trees are planted directly in front of a house entrance or window, they can be destructive and oppressive as they obstruct the flow of incoming *Qi*.

✔ When planted in the West sector, trees block the heat of the setting sun.

✔ A withered or dead tree is a symbol of death and carries *Sha Qi*.

✔ Bamboo and pine trees signify good health and longevity.

✔ Fruit trees like mango and banana trees are not recommended in the garden.

Plants

✔ Plants with healthy green leaves are signs of good nurturing *Qi* and represent the life force of the residents.

✔ Branches and leaves should be cut and trimmed regularly. Do not let overgrown plants block your windows or doors.

✔ Creepers and climber plants should not be allowed to grow over your roof. It is like being trapped under a net.

✔ Dying and sickly plants are bad signs of *Feng Shui* and should be replaced immediately with healthy ones.

✔ Plants with plenty of foliage and those with round leaves are better than those with pointed leaves. It is also inadvisable to grow thorny plants. They produce negative energies and are inauspicious.

Cactus and Bonsai

✔ Cacti have thorns than emit harmful *Sha Qi* and *bonsai* represent stunted growth.

✔ Do not bind *bonsai* with wire. *Bonsai* are a form of life. They are created through cultivation and not by force.

Flower

✔ Flowers represent beauty. They are short-lived but have an immediate effect in enlivening the environment.

✔ Peonies, blossoms and lotuses symbolise good fortune and are ideal for the garden.

✔ It is an excellent idea to combine Wood and Water Elements by displaying a bowl of money plant indoors and water lilies outdoors to activate good energy.

Pets

✔ You can activate the Tortoise sector by keeping some live ones at the back of the garden.

✔ A rooster can substitute for the Phoenix. Avoid keeping birds in cages — it carries the connotation of torture and imprisonment.

✔ Frogs can bring good luck to the occupants, so if you find a toad in your garden, let it be.

Garden Light

✔ Lights bring excellent life-giving *Yang* energy into the garden and can help to balance *Yin* and *Yang* energies.

✔ Place the lights around the boundaries of your garden and switch them on at night.

✔ Lights can be used to enhance the *Qi* of dark and dim corners in the garden.

✔ Lights can be used to harmonise excessive *Yin* energy that may cause the family's luck to dissipate.

✔ A light in the South (Fire) corner of your garden ensures auspicious luck for the family members.

✔ Avoid placing lights in ponds or fountains. The cycle of destruction states that Water is in conflict with Fire, so their close proximity often causes disharmony for the inhabitants.

Rockery

✔ When rockeries are placed such that they block your path, your progress in life will be held up. Therefore, rockeries should not be constructed just in front of your house.

✔ Incorporate a winding pathway into the Dragon side of your garden (left side looking out).

Ponds

✔ Garden ponds are excellent *Feng Shui* features that enhance wealth luck.

✔ Place the pond to the left of your main door (looking out from the house) to support the Green Dragon.

✔ If the pond is placed on the right (the White Tiger side), it may lead to not just wealth, but also extramarital affairs.

✔ To create positive energy, water should be kept running all the time.

✔ Stagnant water creates bad luck and causes problems for the residents.

✔ Invest in a small pump to circulate air in the water and a filter to keep the water clean.

✔ Keeping some fish in the pond will generate additional positive energy.

✔ Ideally, *koi* (carp) are a good recommendation for the pond.

✔ Water lilies and lotuses are both auspicious flowers and can substitute for fish.

✔ To prevent the water in the pond from turning green, it is essential to cover the surface of the pond with floating plants such as water lilies and lotuses.

Fountain

✔ Moving water in the garden is excellent *Feng Shui*. Installation of a water fountain is a good recommendation as it brings the garden to life.

✔ A well-maintained water fountain creates active and positive *Qi*. The sight and sound of moving water creates a soothing ambience for the garden. In business, water fountains are used to generate good profits.

Miniature Waterfall

✔ Miniature waterfalls in the garden landscape are particularly good stimulators of the Water Element, which in turn supports the Wood Element in the East.

✔ Do not construct water features in the South. Doing so will lead to conflict with the Fire Element.

✔ A gentle landscape with flowing water helps to enhance your wealth and career prospects.

Balancing the Five Elements

✔ Water and rocks are complementary partners in the *Feng Shui* garden. An ideal landscape garden beneficial to the inhabitants should comprise a little of each of the Five Elements.

- A pond or fountain symbolising the Water Element

- A copper or bronze feature for the Metal Element

- An abundance of red flowers representing the Fire Element

- Lots of trees and shrubs signifying the Wood Element

- Fertile soil for the Earth Element

Chapter 5

Checklist for Buying a House

✔ The following points form a simple checklist you can use when looking for a new home. You can also apply it to your existing house or workplace.

✔ Note that this is only a guide, and not an exhaustive list of all that a professional *Feng Shui* consultant should consider.

Site
✔ Luxuriant, healthy vegetation and thriving wildlife are signs of a healthy site.

Height
✔ Avoid a building that is located in the shadow of another building, especially when it is opposite your entrance. This deprives your building of sunlight and reduces the amount of *Qi* entering your house.

✔ Avoid a building that is lower than the road, unless it has a basement floor to prop up the living quarters.

Direction

✔ Check that the facing is in harmony with you and your family members.

Main Entrance and Apartment Entrance

✔ In high-rise apartments, the main entrance of the building may not face the same direction as the apartment door. They have different *Feng Shui* implications.

Lighting

✔ Good exposure to sunlight brings more energy into a house and helps keep the energy moving. Therefore, viewing of houses should be carried out in the day.

Sha Qi

✔ Check all doors, windows and other openings for any *Sha Qi* coming in. If there is, attention is needed.

History

✔ Try to find out what happened to the previous owner. A house where the previous owner suffered ill health, divorce or bankruptcy will need attention.

Frequently Asked Questions

✔ How do I know if this is the right house to live in?

✔ Is this house suitable for me and my family?

✔ Is my present house having good or bad *Feng Shui*?

✔ Can the good *Feng Shui* of a house last forever?

✔ How can I improve the *Feng Shui* of my house?

✔ Will renovation works affect the *Feng Shui* of my house?

✔ How do I choose the right house?

Chapter 6

Moving Into a New House

Things to Do

✔ Consult the Chinese almanac to choose a good and auspicious date and time.

Chinese Almanac

✔ The selection of auspicious dates should take into consideration the birth data of the family members, but priority is given to the patriarch.

✔ Two days that are generally regarded as ideal are the 1st and 15th days of each lunar month.

✔ On the day you move in, clean the energies by opening all the windows to let fresh air flow through the house.

✔ Switch on the lights and turn on a tap to signify the flow of energy in the house.

✔ Boil a kettle of water and have a light meal with your family members.

✔ Make sure that you stay for the night after moving in.

Advantages of an Auspicious Home

✔ Living in a house with good *Feng Shui* will make you feel energetic and healthy.

✔ Your career and business paths will be smooth.

✔ Your children will excel academically.

✔ Both husband and wife will find fulfillment in life.

Disadvantages of an Inauspicious Home

✔ A house with bad *Feng Shui* will bring misfortune to its occupants. Opportunities will be scarce and even if there are, you will not be able to take advantage of them.

✔ Sickness can turn fatal for occupants.

✔ Family relations are not harmonious. For instance, children are disobedient and will not perform well in their studies.

PART III:
THE ESSENCE OF
FENG SHUI

Time and Environment

✔ Our environment changes over time, and our attitudes change with the environment.

✔ Time and tide wait for no men.

✔ Good fortune contains little seeds of misfortune. Likewise, the seeds of good fortune are hidden in bad times.

✔ Time moves through cycles of change, transforming good into bad and bad into good.

✔ Living in harmony with the environment is good *Feng Shui*.

✔ However, good *Feng Shui* does not last forever but will change over time.

✔ The *Feng Shui* of a house should be reviewed from time to time.

✔ You can only choose to live with the existing environment or change it with *Feng Shui*.

Yin and Yang

✔ *Yin* and *Yang* are basic principles of dualism in traditional Chinese philosophy. These two opposing yet complementary forces are important to the conceptual way in which Chinese view the universe.

✔ *Yin* and *Yang* are the negative and positive principles that govern the universe. *Yin* and *Yang* have their own attributes and their own magnetic fields of energy.

✔ *Yang* symbolises Heaven, sun, day, brightness, mountain, dragon, male, even, heat and positive whilst *Yin* symbolises Earth, moon, night, darkness, valley, tiger, female, odd, cold and negative.

✔ In *Feng Shui* principles, harmony and balance must be maintained between these two forces.

✔ The energies around us are deemed to be in a beneficial state of balance when both *Yin* and *Yang* are present.

✔ The dwellings of the living must have more *Yang* than *Yin* energy.

✔ *Yin* energy will be in excess when a house is dimly lit, dirty, cluttered, damp and musty.

✔ Open all the windows and doors occasionally to replace the stale energies in the house.

✔ All rooms should have windows to let in natural lighting that can boost the *Yang* energy. Light can also help to balance excessive *Yin* energy in the house.

✔ Everything in the Universe contains varying degrees of *Yin* and *Yang*. Within *Yin* there is a little *Yang* and within *Yang* there is a little *Yin*. Together, they form the *Tai Ji* symbol.

Yin

Yang

Five Elements

✔ Everything within the universe, including human beings, is composed of five basic forces known as the Five Elements.

✔ These energies or intangible forces around us can be divided into Wood, Fire, Earth, Metal and Water.

✔ Each element has its own particular characteristics. They are related to one another through the cycle of birth and the cycle of destruction.

✔ They can be energising or destructive, depending on how they interact with one another.

✔ You can enhance these energies within your own home to activate good *Qi*.

✔ South is related to Fire, North to Water, East to Wood and West to Metal.

✔ Everyone has a particular personal element which is important to him or her. This is known as Self Element.

✔ For example, Wood is important to a person with a weak Fire Element. If you need to activate the Wood Element, place a plant in the East sector of your house to enhance the energy of Wood.

✔ You can also place the plant in the North sector as, according to the Cycle of Birth Theory, Water nourishes the Wood Element.

Cycle of Birth

✔ In this productive cycle, burning of Wood produces Fire, turning into ashes to nourish Earth. The nourishing quality of the Earth produces Metal. Metal in the Earth enriches underground Water, which in turn nourishes vegetation to produce Wood. The Five Elements are thus in a state of harmony.

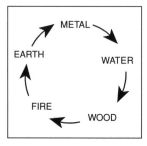

Excerpt from *Hsia Calendar* by Vincent Koh

Cycle of Destruction

✔ In this destructive cycle, Wood penetrates Earth, Earth consumes Water, Water extinguishes the flames and heat of Fire, Fire corrodes Metal, and a sharp Metal blade cuts Wood. The Five Elements are in a state of disharmony.

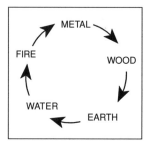

Excerpt from *Hsia Calendar* by Vincent Koh

Colours and the Five Elements

1. Fire - Red, Purple
2. Wood - Green
3. Earth - Brown
4. Metal - White, Gold
5. Water - Blue, Black

Shape of Buildings and the Five Elements

1. Fire Sharp or pointed

2. Wood Tall and slim

3. Earth  Square and flat

4. Metal Round or dome-shaped

5. Water  Curved or corrugated

Eight Characters

✔ To analyse your destiny, you can translate your birth data — the year, month, day and hour of your birth — into the Eight Characters (八字) by using the *Hsia Calendar*, which is also known as the *Thousand Year Calendar*.

✔ These Eight Characters (八字) are also known as the Four Pillars of Destiny. This formula was developed by the ancient Chinese to evaluate and assess the fortune and luck pattern of an individual.

✔ The Eight Characters comprise four pillars, each of which is represented by two elements, written with one above the other. The element on top is the Heavenly Stem and the element below is the Earthly Branch.

✔ Accurate interpretation of the Five Elements within the Eight Characters will be able to unravel the mysteries of how the year, month, day and hour of birth can influence one's life. Accurate analysis enables you to establish the favourable and unfavourable elements within the Eight Characters.

✔ Well-balanced favourable elements in your Eight Characters mean support and harmony in your life. Elements which upset the balance or worsen the imbalance are considered unfavourable.

✔ By analysing the compatibility and incompatibility of the elements within the Eight Characters, an expert in destiny analysis would be able to predict what elements are dominating at a particular time.

✔ The dynamic interaction amongst the Five Elements provides an accurate means of evaluating a person's background, character, business potential, wealth, health, intelligence and social relationships.

✔ The years of good luck that a person encounters during his life is expressed by another set of pillars known as the Luck Pillars. Each set of Luck Pillars consists of two elements, and governs 10 years of a person's life.

✔ By knowing the strengths and weaknesses in your destiny, you can apply *Feng Shui* to make good use of your good years and exercise caution during bad years.

Example

Gender	:	Male
Date of Birth	:	5 February 2000
Time of Birth	:	0030 hrs

The Four Pillars of Destiny (or Eight Characters) and the Luck Pillars of the person above are worked out as shown below.

Hour	Day	Month	Year	
壬H9 +Water	癸H10 -Water (Self)	戊H5 +Earth	庚H7 +Metal	Heavenly Stem
子E1 +Water	巳E6 -Fire	寅E3 +Wood (Season)	辰E5 +Earth	Earthly Branch
			Dragon	Animal Sign

Four Pillars of Destiny

80	70	60	50	40	30	20	10	Starting Age
丙H3 +Fire	乙H2 -Wood	甲H1 +Wood	癸H10 -Water	壬H9 +Water	辛H8 -Metal	庚H7 +Metal	已H6 -Earth	Heavenly Stem
85	75	65	55	45	35	25	15	
戌E11 +Earth	酉E10 -Metal	申E9 +Metal	未E8 -Earth	午E7 +Fire	巳E6 -Fire	辰E5 +Earth	卯E4 -Wood	Earthly Branch

Luck Pillars

Locating the Orientation of an Apartment

✔ In Singapore, about 85% of the population reside in high-rise apartments. Today, with increasing affluence, the designs of apartments have transformed with changing trends and lifestyles. Odd-shaped buildings are increasingly common. How do we identify the facing of such buildings?

Locating the Facing of an Apartment

✔ Facing depends on the entrance to the apartment or the facing of the lift lobby towards the main road.

✔ For high-rise apartments, the entrance to the lobby is the facing of the building and the main door of your flat is the facing of your house. The main door of the apartment (unit) may not necessarily face the same direction as the entrance of the building itself. Both doors have different *Feng Shui* implications.

✔ The facing of the building determines the orientation of the whole block.

Measuring the Orientation

✔ I would suggest that you invest in a compass that provides a reading of 360°. A *Feng Shui* compass, also known as *Luo Pan*, is a more sophisticated tool and is not necessary unless you know its application.

✔ The direction in the *Luo Pan* is given in the form of 24 mountains or 24 directions.

✔ To check the facing direction of an apartment, you should take the reading on the ground floor *outside* the building. This is to avoid magnetic interference from the electrical equipment within the building.

✔ On the ground floor, you should stand approximately three metres away from the building and take the reading from a centralised position facing the main entrance. Make sure you hold your *Luo Pan* horizontally.

✔ Looking at the example on the following page, we see that the back of the building is against North and the front is facing South.

✔ The applicable *Feng Shui* chart for such a building is N - S, which means that the building has its back facing North and its front facing South.

✔ The second step is to discover the facing of the main door to the apartment. Assuming the apartment is on the eighth floor and there are four units on each floor. Stand in front of the relevant unit and take the reading of its main door.

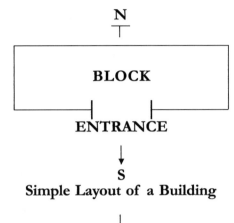

Simple Layout of a Building

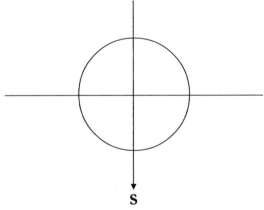

Corresponding Compass Reading
This apartment has a North sitting
and a South facing.

Different apartment units with different door facing lead to different *Feng Shui* interpretations, even if they are in the same building.

✔ Having identified the facing of both the building and the apartment unit, an expert can tell whether the apartment is good or not. An apartment with good *Feng Shui* is not necessarily good for everyone. Similarly, an apartment with deficiency can be corrected by *Feng Shui*. Your Four Pillars of Destiny are crucial for assessing if your house is suitable for you.

✔ There is a Chinese saying that goes: First destiny, second luck and third *Feng Shui*. A person's destiny is established from birth data like his year, month, day and hour of birth. This data is matched against the *Feng Shui* of the apartment.

✔ You can erect your own Four Pillars of Destiny by using the *Hsia Calendar*, of which an English version by this author was published by Asiapac Books. The *Feng Shui* of your apartment would require tools like *Luo Shu* numbers, Eight Trigrams and 24 Mountains.

Luo Shu Numbers

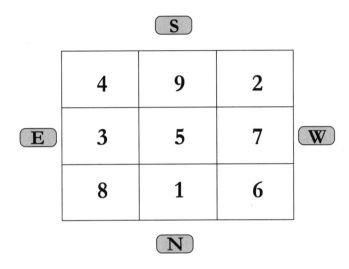

- ✔ The *Luo Shu* square is one of the *Feng Shui* tools for time-dimension analysis.

- ✔ When the *Luo Shu* grid is superimposed onto the *Ba Gua*, the numbers correspond to the Eight Trigrams. See page 103 for more information on the Eight Trigrams.

- ✔ Even numbers — 2, 4, 6 and 8 — are found at each corner of the square grid.

- ✔ Odd numbers — 1, 3, 5, 7 and 9 — are at the four cardinal points, with 5 in the centre.

- ✔ The numbers in the *Luo Shu* grid move, or "fly", in a fixed pattern over time. This movement is referred to as Flying Star Feng Shui.

Flying Stars	Names	Elements	Directions	Relationship
1 White	Tan Lang Xing	Water	North	Travel
2 Black	Ju Men Xing	Earth	South-West	Sickness
3 Green	Lu Cun Xing	Wood	East	Disputes, quarrels
4 Green	Wen Qu Xing	Wood	South-East	Romance, studies
5 Yellow	Lian Zhen Xing	Earth	Centre	Sickness, misfortunes
6 White	Wu Qu Xing	Metal	North-West	Power, legal matters
7 Red	Po Jun Xing	Metal	West	Wealth, prosperity
8 White	Zuo Fu Xing	Earth	North-East	Future prosperity
9 Purple	You Bi Xing	Fire	South	Fire hazard

✔ Presently, the ruling *Luo Shu* number is 7, which reigns from 1984 to 2003.

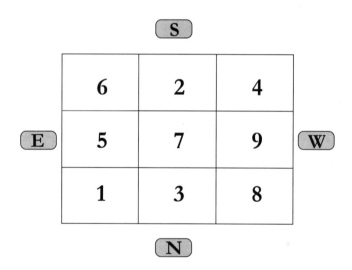

Luo Shu for Age of 7
(Year 1984 - Year 2003)

Eight Trigrams

✔ The Eight Trigrams, or *Ba Gua*, is an octagonal symbol divided into eight sectors. It comprises eight *Gua* (trigrams) grouped around their cosmic progenitors, *Yin* and *Yang*.

✔ The eight sectors of a *Luo Pan* are represented by these trigrams.

✔ Each trigram consists of three combination of continuous or broken lines. We refer to a continuous line (—) as *Yang* and a broken line (- -) as *Yin*.

✔ These trigrams collectively represent the trinity of Heaven, Earth and Man.

✔ The trigram is linked to the *Luo Shu* grid. Together, trigrams and *Luo Shu* numbers formed the foundation for Flying Star analysis.

✔ Each trigram has been assigned a direction, an element and *Yin* or *Yang* characterists according to either the Early Heaven Arrangement or the Later Heaven Arrangement. The difference in the arrangement lies in the placement of the trigrams.

✔ Each trigram has its respective definitions and directions. The distinction between the Early and Later Heaven Arrangement of Trigram is vital to *Feng Shui* analysis.

Qian	-	S
Zhen	-	NE
Kan	-	W
Gen	-	NW
Kun	-	N
Xun	-	SW
Li	-	E
Dui	-	SE

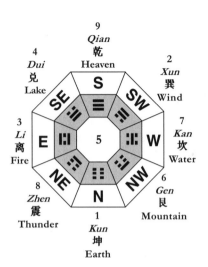

Early Heaven Arrangement in *Luo Shu*

Qian	-	NW
Zhen	-	E
Kan	-	N
Gen	-	NE
Kun	-	SW
Xun	-	SE
Li	-	S
Dui	-	W

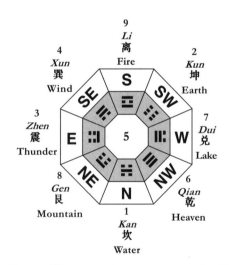

Later Heaven Arrangement in *Luo Shu*

104

Eight Trigrams and Their Relationships in the Later Heaven Arrangement

Luo Shu	Trigrams	Relationships
6	䷀ 乾 *Qian*	North-West, metal, old man, head, heaven
1	☵ 坎 *Kan*	North, water, middle-aged man, ear, winter
8	☶ 艮 *Gen*	North-East, earth, hands, youngest son, mountain
3	☳ 震 *Zhen*	East, eldest son, wood, foot, thunder, spring
4	☴ 巽 *Xun*	South-East, wind, wood, eldest daughter, buttocks
9	☲ 离 *Li*	South, fire, middle-aged woman, eyes, summer
2	☷ 坤 *Kun*	South-West, earth, old woman, stomach
7	☱ 兑 *Dui*	West, metal, young girl, mouth, autumn, lake

Luo Pan

✔ The *Luo Pan* is a Chinese *Feng Shui* compass and is much more complex than its Western maritime counterpart.

✔ The symbols in its various rings indicate good and bad *Feng Shui* definitions and have different meanings for different geomancers.

✔ The *Luo Pan* is used to check the sitting and facing of a house based on the 24 mountains.

✔ Each mountain covers 15°, making a total of 360°.

✔ Houses with different sitting and facing have different *Feng Shui* implications.

✔ A house with bad *Feng Shui* can be corrected by changing the direction of its door.

✔ The size of a *Luo Pan* should not be too small. For accurate reading, a reasonable size is one with a diameter of 180 mm.

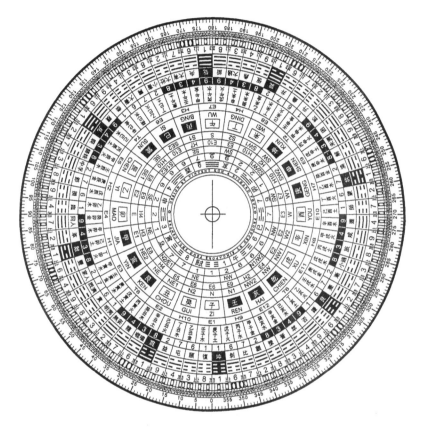

Sample of a *Luo Pan* Designed by
Vincent Koh and Richard Phua

Various Rings of the Luo Pan

Centre   - **Heaven Pool**

1st Ring   - **Credits**
- Designed by Vincent Koh and Richard Phua
- Produced by Singapore Feng Shui Centre

2nd Ring   - **Early Heaven Trigram — *Luo Shu***
- Location of the Eight Palace Theory — based on the sitting
- Water should not be released from these points
- *Luo Shu* numbers

3rd Ring   - **Substitute Stars**
- 3° to either side of the border line (see page 115 for more information)

4th Ring   - **Eight Yellow Water Directions**
- Based on the facing, no water should flow out from these points

5th Ring   - **24 Mountains with Sitting *Sha***
- Based on the sitting

6th Ring   - **24 Directions**
- Eight sectors
- Each sector is divided into three sub-sectors

7th Ring   - **24 Mountains**
- In Chinese characters

8th Ring - **Symbols of 24 Mountains**

8th Ring - **Symbols of 24 Mountains**
- 12 Earthly Branches, 10 Heavenly Stems and Four Trigrams
- Represented by E, H and T respectively

9th Ring - **60 Dragons**

10th Ring - **Early Trigram**
Arranged by *Luo Shu* numbers

11th Ring - **Name of Hexagrams**
- Early Trigram Arrangement

12th Ring - **Permutations of 64 Hexagrams**
- Early Trigram Arrangement

13th Ring - **Flying Stars**
- For Flying Star Theory

14th Ring - **Lines of the Hexagram**
- Six lines of the hexagram
- Red dots are auspicious

15th Ring - **Six Relationships to the Hexagrams**

16th Ring - **360° Reading of Compass**
- The degree position of the 24 Mountains, each covering 15°

24 Mountains

✔ A normal compass is divided into eight sectors: North, South, East, West, North-East, North-West, South-East and South-West.

✔ A *Feng Shui* compass further divides each sector into three sub-sectors, making a total of 24 directions. This division of the compass is also known as the 24 Mountains.

✔ Each sector covers 45° and one sub-sector covers 15°, making a total of 360°.

✔ Houses with different facing and sitting signify different *Feng Shui* characteristics.

✔ Houses are classified into 24 directions, which can have different *Feng Shui* implications.

✔ The 24 mountains are occupied and represented by the 12 Earthly Branches, 10 Heavenly Stems and Four Trigrams.

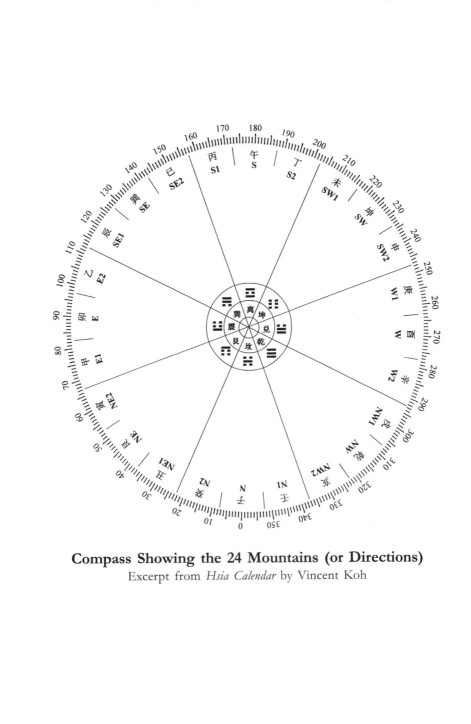

Compass Showing the 24 Mountains (or Directions)

Excerpt from *Hsia Calendar* by Vincent Koh

Directions	Angles (degrees)		Sector
N1	337.5	- 352.5	
N	352.5	- 7.5	North
N2	7.5	- 22.5	
NE1	22.5	- 37.5	
NE	37.5	- 52.5	North-East
NE2	52.5	- 67.5	
E1	67.5	- 82.5	
E	82.5	- 97.5	East
E2	97.5	- 112.5	
SE1	112.5	- 127.5	
SE	127.5	- 142.5	South-East
SE2	142.5	- 157.5	
S1	157.5	- 172.5	
S	172.5	- 187.5	South
S2	187.5	- 202.5	
SW1	202.5	- 217.5	
SW	217.5	- 232.5	South-West
SW2	232.5	- 247.5	
W1	247.5	- 262.5	
W	262.5	- 277.5	West
W2	277.5	- 292.5	
NW1	292.5	- 307.5	
NW	307.5	- 322.5	North-West
NW2	322.5	- 337.5	

Earthly Branches

✔ The 12 Earthly Branches are used to calculate the seasons, years, months, days and time in the Lunar Calendar. They are assigned an element and direction each as shown in the *Luo Pan*. They are represented by the 12 animal signs.

E1	子	Rat	(+Water)	E7	午 Horse	(+Fire)
E2	丑	Ox	(-Earth)	E8	未 Ram	(-Earth)
E3	寅	Tiger	(+Wood)	E9	申 Monkey	(+Metal)
E4	卯	Rabbit	(-Wood)	E10	酉 Rooster	(-Metal)
E5	辰	Dragon	(+Earth)	E11	戌 Dog	(+Earth)
E6	巳	Snake	(-Fire)	E12	亥 Pig	(-Water)

Note that (-) represents *Yin* and (+) represents *Yang*.

Heavenly Stems

✔ The 10 Heavenly Stems and also linked to the Five Elements — Water, Wood, Fire, Earth and Metal. Heavenly Stems show the pattern of movement of the Heaven *Qi*. Heavenly Stems are used to represent the state of *Qi* in the Universe. Each year is represented by a Heavenly Stem and an Earthly Branch.

HI	甲	(+Wood)	H6	己	(-Earth)
H2	乙	(-Wood)	H7	庚	(+Metal)
H3	丙	(+Fire)	H8	辛	(-Metal)
H4	丁	(-Fire)	H9	壬	(+Water)
H5	戊	(+Earth)	H10	癸	(-Water)

Note that (-) represents *Yin* and (+) represents *Yang*.

✔ Likewise, a person's birth data can be represented by the Heavenly Stems and Earthly Branches, and is used in the

Four Pillars Of Destiny analysis. An expert can even read a person's character, luck pattern and relationship with others from the birth data.

Trigrams
✔ The remaining Four Mountains are represented by four of the Eight Trigrams.

Kun ☷ at SW   *Qian* ☰ at NW

Xun ☴ at SE   *Gen* ☶ at NE

Substitute Stars

✔ The compass is divided into the 24 Mountains or directions, each of which covers 15°. If we further divide each mountain into sub-sectors of 3° each, we have five sub-sectors in every Mountain.

✔ In Flying Star Feng Shui analysis, if the facing of the house lies on the outer sub-sector of a mountain, we apply the Substitute Flying Star theory to analyse the *Feng Shui* of the house.

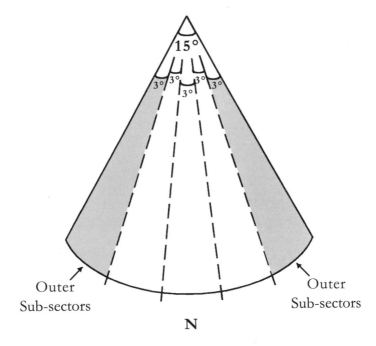

Five Sub-sectors Within a Mountain

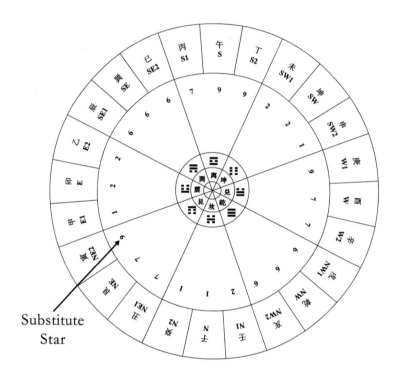

Substitute
Star

Compass Showing the Substitute Stars
Excerpt from *Hsia Calendar* by Vincent Koh

Angles Within the Deviation for Substitute Stars

		Mountain	Mid-point Degrees	Sub-sector Limit
壬	Ren	N1	345	340.5 - 349.5
子	Zi	N	0	355.5 - 4.5
癸	Gui	N2	15	10.5 - 19.5
丑	Chou	NE1	30	25.5 - 34.5
艮	Gen	NE	45	40.5 - 49.5
寅	Yin	NE2	60	55.5 - 64.5
甲	Jia	E1	75	70.5 - 79.5
卯	Mao	E	90	85.5 - 94.5
乙	Yi	E2	105	100.5 - 109.5
辰	Chen	SE1	120	115.5 - 124.5
巽	Xun	SE	135	130.5 - 139.5
巳	Si	SE2	150	145.5 - 154.5
丙	Bing	S1	165	160.5 - 169.5
午	Wu	S	180	175.5 - 184.5
丁	Ding	S2	195	190.5 - 199.5
未	Wei	SW1	210	205.5 - 214.5
坤	Kun	SW	225	220.5 - 229.5
申	Shen	SW2	240	235.5 - 244.5
庚	Geng	W1	255	250.5 - 259.5
酉	You	W	270	265.5 - 274.5
辛	Xin	W2	285	280.5 - 289.5
戌	Xu	NW1	300	295.5 - 304.5
乾	Qian	NW	315	310.5 - 319.5
亥	Hai	NW2	330	325.5 - 334.5

Grand Duke

✔ The Grand Duke (太岁) is a yearly ruling star.

✔ Never sit in a position opposite the Grand Duke. Facing the Grand Duke brings disaster, misfortune and defeat.

✔ The location and direction of the Grand Duke corresponds to the 12 zodiac animals in the lunar year.

✔ In the year of Dragon the Grand Duke is in the SE1 sector, 112.5° - 127.5°.

Feng Shui Advice

✔ During the year when your main door faces the Grand Duke, avoid carrying out any major renovation works.

✔ Take note of when you will be in conflict with the Grand Duke. For example, those born in the year of Dog are said to be in conflict with the Grand Duke in the year of Dragon.

✔ Avoid taking high risks in your business during a year when you are in conflict with the Grand Duke.

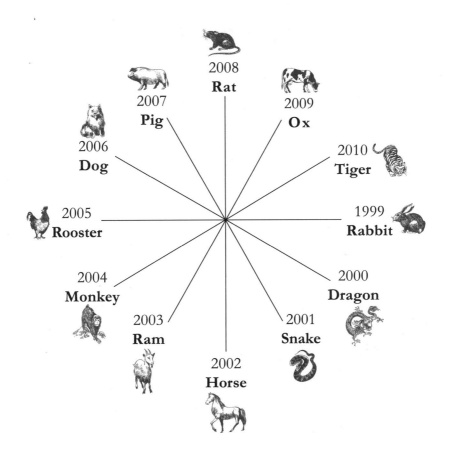

Location of the Grand Duke

Zodiac animals from Vincent Koh's
Hsia Calendar, illustrated by Jeffrey Seow

Three Killings

✔ The Three Killings (三煞) is another inauspicious yearly ruling star.

✔ The Three Killings location is in the West during the year of Rabbit, Ram and Pig.

✔ The Three Killings location is in the South during the year of Dragon, Monkey and Rat.

✔ The Three Killings location is in the East during the year of Snake, Rooster and Ox.

✔ The Three Killings location is in the North during the year of Horse, Dog and Tiger.

Feng Shui Advice

✔ Do not sit with the Three Killings behind your back. You may, however, face the Three Killings direction.

✔ You may start renovation works in the sector opposite the Three Killings.

✔ In the year 2000, the Three Killings is in the South.

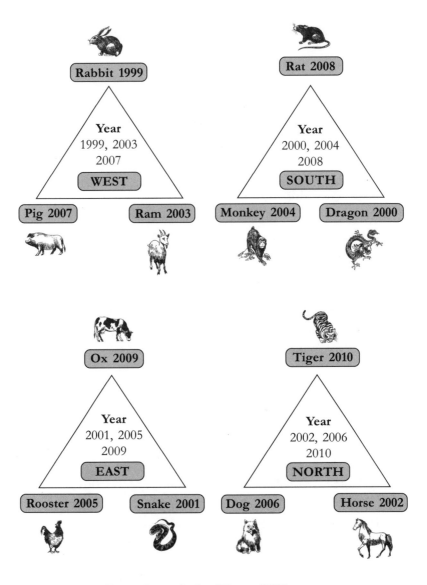

Location of the Three Killings

Zodiac animals from Vincent Koh's
Hsia Calendar, illustrated by Jeffrey Seow

Flying Star Feng Shui

✔ Flying Star Feng Shui addresses the time dimension of *Feng Shui* and the movement of energy around the house.

✔ This method offers a specific way of drawing up the natal chart of every house and is used to analyse the unseen energies within the house.

✔ A natal chart is made up of a collection of numbers, all set within a grid. These numbers and their combination within the grid can forecast specific events.

✔ The natal chart can calculate the luck and happenings in every sector of a house, in any given month and year for a 20-year period.

✔ With it, you can establish the potential for wealth, prosperity and harmonious relations in your house, as well as detect negative energies and unseen influences.

✔ It can also point out the family members who have the greatest potential to take advantage of good fortune.

✔ It can warn family members to avoid misfortune like sickness, scandals or legal entanglement.

✔ This method is excellent for warning against potent Flying Stars that bring bad luck to the occupants of the house.

4 Wood	9 Fire	2 Earth
3 Wood	5 Earth	7 Metal
8 Earth	1 Water	6 Metal

✔ The *Feng Shui* of a house is influenced by the external environment, which is divided into tangible and intangible forces around us. The tangible environment encompasses the forms and shapes around us, like buildings, doors and windows. The intangible environment refers to unseen influences like Flying Stars.

✔ These unseen influences all around us are called *Qi* or life force. *Qi* is described in the context of *Yin* and *Yang* energies or Five Elements — Metal, Water, Wood, Fire and Earth.

✔ Flying Star Feng Shui is complex but is commonly

practised in Asia. It was revived in Hong Kong at the start of the Cultural Revolution, when it was illegal to practise *Feng Shui* and religion in China. Many *Feng Shui* masters left the mainland and relocated to Hong Kong, Taiwan, Malaysia and Singapore, where they could practise *Feng Shui* openly.

✔ Flying Star Feng Shui is sophisticated and dynamic. It has specific theories to calculate the movements and changes of the energy around us. It is the only *Feng Shui* technique which studies the temporal changes taking place in a house.

✔ For instance, what type of fortune does your house have? Does it have good potential for prosperity and fortune? Which family members will benefit and for how long? With Flying Star Feng Shui, all these questions can be answered.

✔ Knowing the good locations within your house, a *Feng Shui* analyst can assist you in designing the interior layout of your living room, bedrooms, kitchen and bathrooms. Similarly, you can also avoid the bad locations within the house which are not suitable for you.

✔ With expert analysis, benign energies can be activated to enhance the prosperity, wealth and health sectors within your house, while hostile energies are avoided and harmonised to avoid misfortune and illness.

✔ Besides singling out family members with the greatest potential to take advantage of good fortune, Flying Star Feng Shui can also advise family members to avoid negative energies which may otherwise bring sickness, scandals and legal problems to them.

✔ The Flying Star method is perfect for applying to houses at the planning stage. With expert analysis, it is possible to ensure that the house is designed to face the most favourable and auspicious direction.

✔ Based on the natal chart of the house, ensure that the rooms are distributed according to the individual ruling elements of each occupant.

✔ This technique can also be used in the interior design stage, particularly on colour schemes and the layout of furniture and fixtures suitable for each individual member. Houses designed according to *Feng Shui* principles will attract and enhance wealth and career luck.

✔ Flying Star Feng Shui has the ability to examine the occurrence of events in your house and to reveal its past, present and future potential. It enables a *Feng Shui* consultant to analyse the quality of energies and influences currently affecting your house, thereby manipulating them to your advantage.

Three Periods and Nine Ages

✔ Apart from the space dimension, *Feng Shui* also has a time dimension. *Feng Shui* divides time into three periods. Each period comprises three ages, each lasting 20 years, making a total of 180 years to complete one full cycle.

	Upper Period	Age of 1 (1864 - 1883)
		Age of 2 (1884 - 1903)
		Age of 3 (1904 - 1923)
A Cycle	Middle Period	Age of 4 (1924 - 1943)
		Age of 5 (1944 - 1963)
		Age of 6 (1964 - 1983)
	Lower Period	Age of 7 (1984 - 2003)
		Age of 8 (2004 - 2023)
		Age of 9 (2024 - 2043)

✔ Age of 7 began in 1984 and will last until the year 2003. Age of 8 will reign from year 2004 for the next 20 years and so on.

✔ The Flying Star Chart, depending on the direction and facing of a house, gives an indication of how the intangible forces are distributed during each age. It is the basic guide for drawing up a birth chart of any building completed at any age.

Mountain Stars and Water Stars

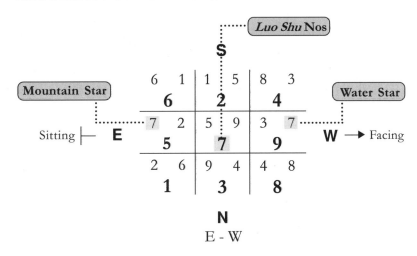

**Flying Star Chart of a House Sitting
East and Facing West in Age of 7**

✔ Look at the Flying Star Chart above. In each square are
three numbers. The smaller number in the top left corner
is the Mountain Star. The smaller number on the right is
the Water Star. The larger number is a *Luo Shu* number.

✔ Mountain Stars control and affect a person's health and
descendants. Water Stars control wealth, career and
harmony. If a house faces a good Water Star, it will bring
harmony and prosperity to the people living there. If the
main door of the house faces a bad Water Star, it will create
disharmony and problems in the house.

✔ Prosperous Stars during Age of 7 (1984 - 2003) are 7, 8 and
9. A house sitting on a good Mountain Star (7) and facing
a prosperous Water Star (7) has a good configuration and
will bring harmony and prosperity to its occupants.

How to Use the Flying Star Chart

✔ A birth chart of a house can be drawn up on the basis of its direction and the age during which the building is completed. The Flying Star Chart shows the distribution of intangible *Feng Shui* influence in relation to the house.

✔ Below is a birth chart of a house completed in the year 1999. The back and front face NE1 and SW1 respectively.

✔ This birth chart is then superimposed on the floorplan of a house to analyse the strengths and weaknesses of the house. This is demonstrated on the following page.

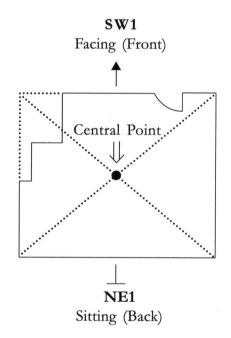

SW1
Facing (Front)

NE1
Sitting (Back)

**Birth Chart of a House Completed
in 1999 During Age of 7**

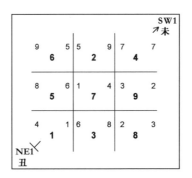

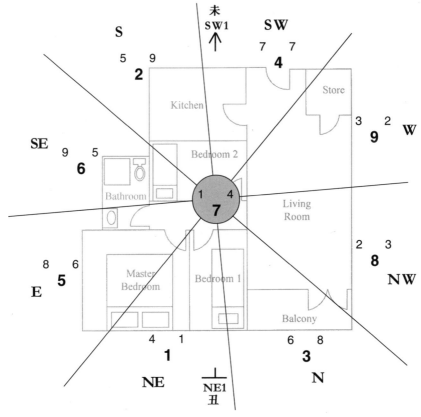

**Flying Star Chart Showing the Distribution of
Water and Mountain Stars in Each Sector of a House**
Excerpt from *Hsia Calendar* by Vincent Koh

Yearly Flying Star Chart

✔ The yearly Flying Star Chart shows the movement of the nine stars on the *Luo Shu* grid. The Flying Stars are assigned numbers from 1 to 9.

✔ The stars move in a fixed pattern and change in relation to time. Every year there is a ruling star. For example, in the year 2000, the ruling star is 9.

✔ During the period from 1984 to 2003, the two potent stars are 2 and 5. These are sickness stars. Houses in confrontation with these two stars will see sickness and misfortune.

✔ Referring to Yearly Flying Star Charts, we note that, in the year 2000, the bad star 5 is in the North and star 2 is in the West.

✔ If your main door faces Star 2 or 5 in a particular year, precaution should be exercised. Stars 2 and 5 are of Earth Element and can be harmonised by using a metal object to dissolve the *Sha Qi*.

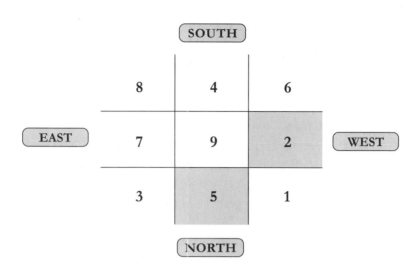

**Chart Showing the Energy Moving
Around Us During the Year 2000**

Star	Element	Star	Element
1	Water	5	Earth
2	Earth	6	Metal
3	Wood	7	Metal
4	Wood	8	Earth
		9	Fire

Checklist of a Feng Shui Adviser

Flying Star Chart

✔ Check to ensure that the Flying Star Chart is drawn according to the sitting and facing of the building.

✔ Check that the layout plan is drawn to scale.

✔ From the Flying Star Chart, check the sector that the main entrance is in as this determines the quality of the house.

✔ Check the respective furnishings in the house and record on the layout plan.

✔ Take note of critical areas that require attention.

✔ Based on the Flying Star Chart for the current year, advise the client of any future actions that are necessary.

Main door   Kitchen

Sitting room

Master
bedroom

Bathroom

Garden

Birth Data Analysis

✔ Check that all the family members' birth data are correct.

✔ Erect the Four Pillars of Destiny.

✔ Check their favourable elements, facing, directions and colour schemes.

✔ Explain your findings to your clients and check with them on the accuracy of the findings. If everything is in order, proceed with the *Feng Shui* cures.

Recommendations

✔ Make sure any required alteration to the house is safe and can be approved by relevant authorities.

✔ Check for simple and economical cures.

✔ Any *Feng Shui* recommendations must be practical and should not cause inconvenience to the client.

Written by Vincent Koh
Unveil Your Destiny helps you to make sense of the highly-condensed data in your Eight Characters. This book picks up where the author's first book, *Hsia Calendar*, left off and show you how to draw conclusions about your own destiny.

Written by Vincent Koh
For the first time, the Hsia Calendar is now available in English to guide you into the world of Feng Shui. Complete with symbols, this book will enable you to erect your personal Pillars of Destiny or Eight Characters, live in harmony with your environment and avert disaster.

Written & illustrated in comics by Tan Xiaochun
I Ching is often seen as a storehouse of wisdom for guidance on the conduct of life. This book seeks to remove the mystique surrounding the I Ching, and offers a quick look at the origins and applications of the I Ching.

Written by Sherman Tai. Illustrated in comics by Wee See Heng
This book explains the basic principles of Feng Shui and how they work. Discover the ancient Chinese mystical art of placement at work to create a situation where good or bad fortune becomes the order of the day.

Basic Science of Feng Shui

Written by Vincent Koh

Previously perceived to be an inaccessible subject, the burgeoning interest in authentic Feng Shui over the years has led to an explosion of Feng Shui guides. Every now and then, an authentic classic comes along to illuminate the world of Feng Shui. This book does just that.

Rigorously researched, *Basic Science of Feng Shui: A Handbook for Practitioners* is no bedtime read for the average Feng Shui fan. It elucidates the theories and applications of authentic Feng Shui. The Flying Star, Substitute Star and Water Theories have also been presented in a concise manner that provides practitioners with a true understanding of the complex formulae and practical application involved.

Though tailored to be an indispensable guide for Feng Shui practitioners, this well-organised and clearly-written book will be an enlightening read for Feng Shui beginners too. Your journey to delve into the science of Feng Shui starts here.

Important concepts covered include the following:
* Eight Trigrams
* Eight House Theory
* Flying Star Analysis
* Flying Star Charts (Age 1 to Age 9)
* Substitute Star Application
* Substitute Star Charts (Age 1 to Age 9)
* Water Theories
* Feng Shui Audit

BASIC SCIENCE OF
Feng Shui
A Handbook for Practitioners
Vincent Koh
ASIAPAC PUBLICATION

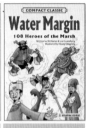

新千禧年风水

编著 ： 许锦华
绘画 ： 林明华

亚太图书有限公司出版